W9-BKA-264

Me and My World

On the Move

Sue Barraclough

WINDMILL
BOOKS

Published in 2009 in the United States by Windmill Books, LLC
303 Park Avenue South, Suite #1280, New York, NY 10010-3657

U.S. publication copyright © Wayland Publishing 2009
First North American edition

Design and typography: Natascha Frensch Read Regular
(European Community Design Registration 2008)
Read Regular and Read Xheavy copyright
© Natascha Frensch 2001-2007

Publisher Cataloging Data

Barraclough, Sue
    On the move / Sue Barraclough.
        p.   cm.—(Me and my world)
    Includes index.
    Summary: Simple text and photographs introduce
    transportation vehicles, including scooters, buses, trucks,
    motorcycles, and airplanes.
    ISBN 978-1-60754-058-8 (library binding)
    ISBN 978-1-60754-064-9 (paperback)
    ISBN 978-1-60754-065-6 (6-pack)
1. Transportation—Juvenile literature [1. Transportation 2. Vocabulary]
I. Title   II. Series
    388—dc22

Manufactured in China

Photo Credits: Cover © Franck Seguin/TempSport/Corbis; p1, 17 © George Hall/Corbis;
pp 2-3 © Creasource/Corbis; pp 4-5, 22 Lori Adamski Peek/Stone/Getty; p 6, 22 © Jim Cummins/
Corbis; p 7 © Mina Chapman/Corbis; pp 8-9 © Vince Streano/Corbis; p 10, 22 © Ron Watts/Corbis;
pp 12-13 © Neil Rabinowitz/Corbis; pp 14-15 © Armin Weigel/dpa/Corbis; p 16 © Franck Seguin/
TempSport/Corbis; p 19, 22 Lester Lefkowitz/The Image Bank/Getty; pp 20-21 Hans Wolf/
The Image Bank/Getty.

Contents

running

The children are **running**.

Running is a way to move around.

scooter

This is a **scooter**.

The boy zooms down the hill on his **scooter**.

bicycle

This is a **bicycle**.

The **bicycle** moves fast!

bus

This is a bus.

The children are waiting for the bus.

truck

This is a truck.

The truck moves some
heavy wood.

11

helicopter

This is a helicopter.

This helicopter is landing on a beach.

tractor

This is a **tractor**.

The **tractor** moves slowly down the field.

motorcycles

These are **motorcycles**.

The **motorcycles** are in a race.

plane

This is a plane.

The plane flies high in the sky.

train

This is a train.

A train moves along tracks.

traffic

This is a **traffic** jam.

20

The cars and trucks cannot move!

Picture Quiz Game

Can you find these things in the book?

hat

helmet

tracks

wood

What pages are they on?

Index Quiz Game

The index is on page 24.
Use the index to help you
answer these questions.

1. Which page shows a truck?
   What color is the truck?

2. Which pages show children running?
   How many children are there?

3. Which page shows motorcycle?
   What number is on the first motorcycle?

4. Which page shows a tractor?
   What color is the field?

Index and Web Sites

Answers

Picture Quiz Game: The hat is on page 4, the helmet is on page 6, the tracks are on page 19, the wood is on page 10.
Index Quiz Game: 1. page 10, yellow; 2. pages 4-5, five; 3. page 16, number 3; 4. page 15, green and brown.

Web Sites
To ensure the currency and safety of recommended Internet links, Windmill maintains and updates an online list of sites related to the subject of this book. To access this list of Web sites, please go to www.windmillbooks.com/weblinks and select this book's title.

For more great fiction and nonfiction, go to windmillbooks.com.